The Ultimate Scale Book

by Troy Stetina

CONTENTS

What are Scales?

Scales are simply collections of notes used in music. We call a set of notes a *scale* when we extract the notes from their musical setting and arrange them in order from a starting point. When left in their musical context, these same notes are called a *key*. So scales and keys are essentially the same thing. The difference is simply an issue of application—you can think of scales as the theoretical "residue" of music.

Why are they important? Having an understanding of scales will greatly enhance your overall musical development. It will help you to spontaneously improvise solos as well as to develop better relative pitch discrimination (and the associated skill of learning music "by ear"). Furthermore, you will find that different scales evoke different moods, and certain scales are common to certain styles of music. Eventually, you will learn to recognize the scales purely by their distinctive sounds.

In a nutshell, understanding scales, their interrelationships, and their tonal construction is the essence of learning the fretboard.

Two Sides to the Story

Scales have two different and important aspects: *tonality* and *modality*.

Tonality refers to the pitch of the starting note, or "root" note. For example, A major and G major demonstrate two different tonalities. Different tonalities may also be called simply "different keys."

Modality refers to the relative structure of the pitches based on a given root note. For example, A major and A Phrygian describe two different modalities both beginning on the same pitch of A. Modalities may be referred to as being different "types of keys."

So any scale or key requires two things to be specified—a starting pitch (tonality), and a type of scale (modality). When a player says a certain song is in the "key of A," this could in fact mean A major, A Mixolydian, A minor, etc. In practice, the modality—or type of key—is often understood based upon the style.

Further Down the Road

Many styles of music may blend or borrow between modalities. The blues, for example, commonly utilizes a minor pentatonic (or blues) scale played over a major-type background. I mention this simply to emphasize the fact that scales are not inviolate "rules" that must be obeyed. They are simply useful collections of notes that may be blended or modified as needed. But of course, we must first learn the scales separately before we start combining them!

How to Learn Scales

This book can function as a reference, where you look up a particular scale and learn its fretboard pattern as needed, but it is also structured as a "scale method." That is, if you start at the beginning and learn each scale in the order presented, you will find that they build in a logical and systematic sequence.

Learning these scales is a process that will take some time and practice. Don't pressure yourself to learn them too quickly, as this will only cause you to confuse one with the next. Instead, spend enough time with one pattern until you can play through it repeatedly without mistakes. And play slowly! This isn't a race. After you are comfortable with a given scale, continue to review it from time to time, even as you move on to memorize the next scale pattern.

Now a word about how to practice scales. Obviously one can simply play up and down until the pattern "sinks in." However, repeating a scale ad nauseum is generally not a particularly effective strategy because the amount of repetition required is often more than any sane person can take! Therefore, it is best to apply a variety of approaches. Here are a few ideas to keep things a bit more interesting:

- Start with the lowest note and add one note at a time, cycling ever higher and higher until you are playing up and down the full scale pattern.

- Sequence the scale ascending and descending in groups of two, three, and four, etc.

- Playing to a metronome, improvise within the scale while maintaining constant eighth or sixteenth notes. You may draw upon sequences, make contours, or skip notes, but don't leave the scale!

Some of the possible sequences are demonstrated on the first few scales. Of course, you should continue to apply them to each of the scales presented.

Finally, it is important to realize that for scales to ultimately be learned effectively, you must see them at work in real life situations. Then, you will really know them! All theoretical knowledge, including scales, is useless without application. So it is recommended that as you progress through this book, you learn enough music, songs, and/or solos to see some application of these patterns. If this is difficult for you, you may find it beneficial to seek out private lessons with a teacher who can help you recognize real musical applications for each scale.

Reading Fretboard Diagrams

The scales in this book are presented using fretboard diagrams that work like a picture of the guitar neck. These diagrams reflect the neck from the *player's view*. That is, they show the same string and fret placement that you see when you look down at your guitar neck (high E string on top, low E string on the bottom).

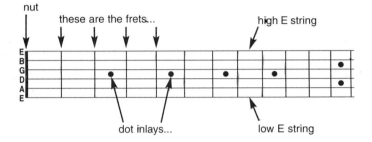

The dots, or inlays, on the neck of your guitar appear on frets 3, 5, 7, 9, and double dots appear at fret 12 (one octave above the open strings). Then above the twelfth fret, the same pattern repeats. In diagrams, these dots are replaced with the actual fret numbers.

| | 3 | 5 | 7 | 9 | 12 | 15 | 17 | 19 | 21 |

Smaller portions of the fretboard diagram are often used to focus attention on a certain area. For example, the diagram below depicts just the area of the neck between the fifth and ninth frets.

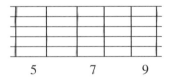

Dots are used on the fretboard "grid" to indicate the fingering locations notes. Root notes are indicated by circled dots.

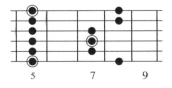

6

A Word About Fingerings

Fingerings are never "written in stone," but it is generally a good idea to select one and stick with it for a given scale pattern.

Positional Fingering

Positional fingering is a good starting point. This means that each finger gets one fret and plays all notes in that fret. The position number is the fret number of the first, or index finger.

For example, the scale shown at the bottom of the previous page (A minor pentatonic) is in *fifth position*. The C major scale shown at the bottom of the following page is in *seventh position*.

One special case is *open position* which is synonymous with first position.

> • Position is not always the lowest fret used in a pattern, but rather the lowest fret of the *majority* of notes in the pattern. So if all notes are in eighth position except one note on one string which lies on the seventh fret, the pattern is in *eighth position*, not seventh position. Simply stretch your index finger back one fret when required.

"Blues" Fingering

An alternate fingering approach common to pentatonic-based styles which incorporate a lot of string bending (such as blues and rock) favors fingers 1 and 3, or the index and ring fingers. This often requires an extra stretch here or there, and can be viewed as a modification to the positional approach.

Shifting-Type Fingering

Some scale patterns will require sliding, or shifting, the hand position, so that two different notes on the same string are played with the same finger. Specific directions will indicate how this can be best achieved for each pattern on an individual basis.

Additionally, other scales may involve the use of a "floating position" where the pattern begins in one position, then on a particular string, the position shifts into a different position. This happens, for example, in diatonic three-note-per-string patterns.

Construction Basics

Historically speaking, the major scale is the fundamental scale in Western music. It is a *diatonic* (seven-tone) scale formed by a specific sequence of whole (two fret) and half (one fret) steps. It is easiest to remember the sequence if you view it as two "whole-whole-half" patterns, separated by a whole step.

W   W   H | W   W   H
                   W

When this is applied to a string on the fretboard, the major scale emerges. Below, the starting note (or *root*) is C, so this is a C major scale, played all on one string.

C major

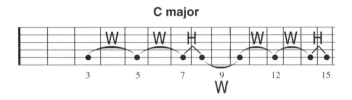

The steps of a major scale are numbered 1–2–3–4–5–6–7. (The octave root may be shown as either 8 or 1.) Half steps appear between tones 3–4 and 7–8. All other steps are whole steps.

C major

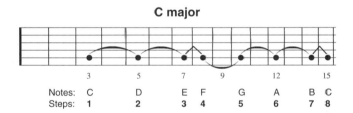

Notes:	C	D	E	F	G	A	B	C
Steps:	1	2	3	4	5	6	7	8

When the major scale is "collapsed" and played across the neck rather than on a single string, the common single-octave major shape below emerges. Play it in seventh position. (Notes on the 7th fret are played with your index finger.) The root note—C, steps 1 and 8—is shown with circled dots.

C major

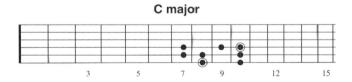

- Other tonalities are formed by shifting the whole pattern to begin on other root notes, but the relative spacing and the numbers for any major scale always remain the same, and reflect each tone's intervallic relationship to the root.

All other scales may be viewed as being alterations of the major scale. For example, the minor pentatonic scale (a common five-tone minor scale) omits the 2nd and 6th steps, and flats the 3rd step (a *minor* 3rd) and the 7th step (a *minor* 7th).

major (diatonic) tones:	1	2	3	4	5	6	7
minor pentatonic tones:	1		♭3	4	5		♭7

Below, the minor pentatonic pattern is shown starting on the note C. Notice the three-fret intervals between the root–♭3rd and 5th–♭7th. These give the pentatonic scale a distinctly more aggressive character as compared to the diatonic scale

C minor pentatonic

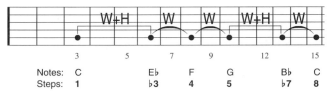

Notes:	C	E♭	F	G	B♭	C
Steps:	1	♭3	4	5	♭7	8

When played across the neck, this common single-octave minor pentatonic shape emerges. Play it in eighth position (notes on the 8th fret are played with your index finger).

C minor pentatonic

PART I

Minor Pentatonic

The minor pentatonic scale is a five-tone minor scale common in blues, rock, pop, funk and other styles. We'll start with the common tonality of E. Here are the notes, tones, and intervallic structure.

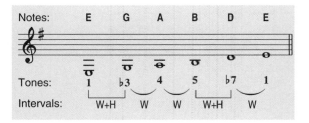

E minor pentatonic, boxes 1 – 5

The patterns are often called *boxes* because of their two-note-per-string shapes. Notice that box 1 includes all the open strings.

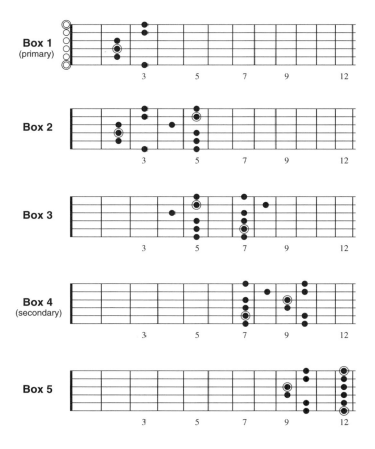

Fingering: Box 1 is in *open position*, box 2 is in *second position*, box 3 is in *fifth position* (stretch back a fret on the G string), box 4 is in *seventh position*, and box 5 is in *ninth position*. An alternate approach is to use fingers 1 and 3 for each pattern (except open). Or you may combine them, playing the lower (wider) frets with positional fingering, and the higher (narrower) frets with fingers 1 and 3.

Here is how they all fit together. Play up box 1, down 2, up 3, down 4, and up 5. Then reverse it and come back down. Do this until the whole sequence is memorized. The staff-tab below will get you started.

- The top of box 1 forms the bottom of box 2, the top of box 2 forms the bottom of box 3, etc.

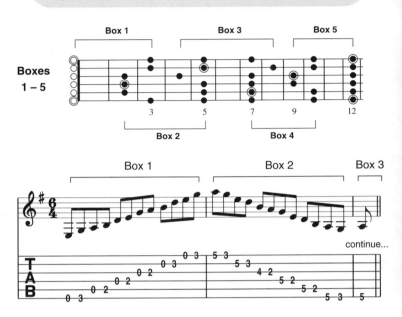

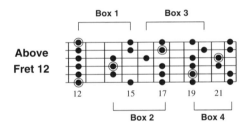

continue...

Above box 5, the patterns continue starting again with box 1. The shapes are exactly the same, with everything shifted up twelve frets.

If you put these two sections together, you have the entire neck! Although at first glance this may look like a bit of a mess, if you have already memorized the shapes and sequence, you'll find nothing new here.

- To find specific boxes more quickly, use the E minor chords in boxes 1 and 4, shown in the bottom diagram, as "anchor points."

E minor pentatonic, full neck

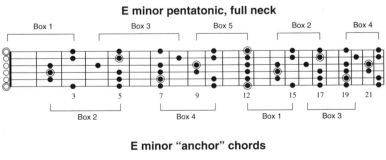

E minor "anchor" chords

E minor pentatonic, diagonal shapes

The minor pentatonic scale may also be played in *diagonal* shapes which cut across several boxes. The most common diagonal shapes of E minor pentatonic are centered on boxes 1 and 4.

Here is E minor pentatonic box 1, or the primary box, shown first with its low extension (into box 5), then with its high extension (into box 2), and finally, the full diagonal shape.

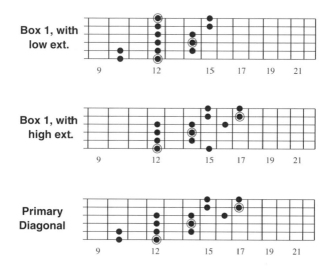

Here is E minor pentatonic box 4, or secondary box, first with its low extension (into box 3 and lower), then with its high extension (into box 5), and finally, the full diagonal shape.

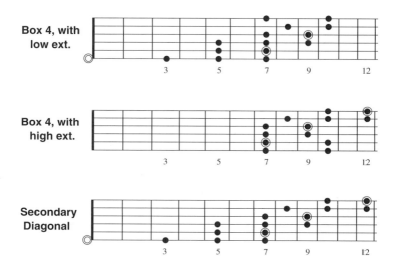

Fingering: These diagonal shapes involve shifting positions. As a rule, try playing all notes available in a given position before you shift positions. So playing the first example above (Box 1) from the lowest note, you would begin in tenth position and use the fingering 1-3-1-3, then shift into twelfth position and play the next note with your third finger. Reverse this for descending.

Other tonalities

Now we'll consider other tonalities. This simply requires that the entire series of boxes is shifted up or down the neck. While shifting just one or two frets is easily accomplished, shifting three or more frets can become confusing. Therefore, it is a good idea to memorize at least the common keys shown here. First play the anchor chords shown under the series of boxes to get your "bearings," then play up and down the boxes over the entire neck in that key.

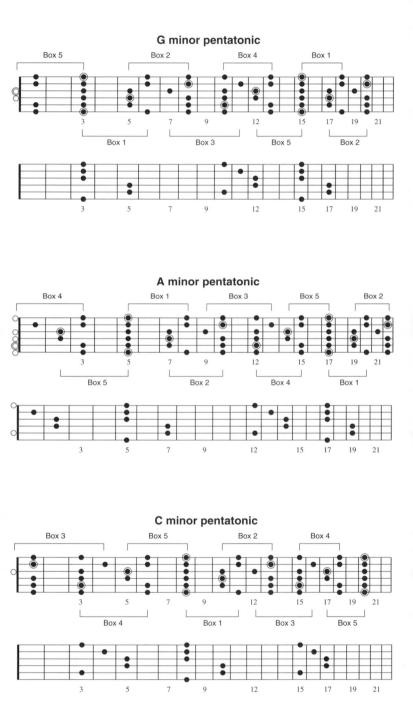

At this point, you have learned the minor pentatonic scale in E, G, A, and C. For the remaining "in between" keys—F, F♯, G♯, B♭, B, C♯, D, and D♯—simply take the nearest key and slide up or down a fret or two, to place the root of the pattern on the correct pitch. (See page 63 for note names on the neck, if necessary.)

13

Sequencing practice

Several different sequence patterns are applied to a few minor pentatonic scales to help get you started with this practice concept. Apply each of these sequences to each of the minor pentatonic scale patterns learned so far in all the various keys.

E minor pentatonic, box 1, sequenced in threes, ascending

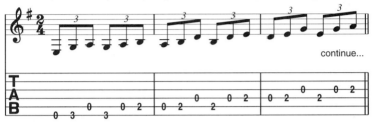

continue...

E minor pentatonic, box 2, sequenced in threes, descending

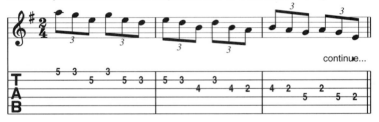

continue...

A minor pentatonic, box 1, sequenced in fours, descending

continue...

A minor pentatonic, box 2, sequenced in fours, ascending

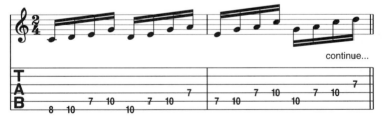

continue...

C minor pentatonic, box 4, in "backward" threes, ascending

continue...

Blues

The blues scale is a six-tone minor scale common in blues, rock, and other contemporary styles. It is almost identical to the minor pentatonic, except for one added tone—a flatted 5th. Here are the notes, tones, and intervallic structure shown based on E.

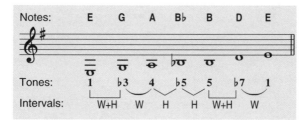

E blues, boxes 1 – 5

If you have already learned the minor pentatonic scale, the blues scale is a piece of cake. The minor pentatonic is shown in solid dots with the added ♭5th in grey.

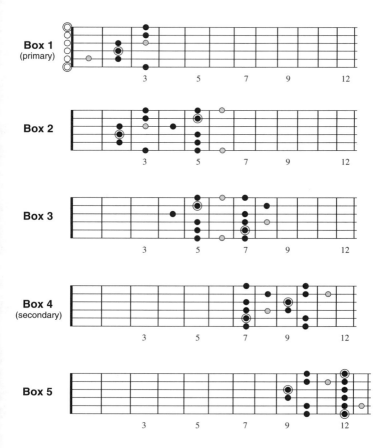

Fingering: Box 1 uses *open position*. Box 2 shifts between *third and second position*, then back to third position for strings 1 and 2. Box 3 is in *fifth position* (stretch back a fret on the G string). Box 4 is in *seventh position* (up to eighth position for string 2). Box 5 is in *tenth position* (stretch back a fret on strings 3 and 4). Alternatively, you may simply use fingers 1 and 3 except when an extra finger is required due to having three notes on a string.

Below are all five interconnected boxes for E blues. Play through each pattern, shifting up and down the neck. Then practice using the sequence patterns from page 14. Remember to visualize the E minor "anchor" chords within boxes 1 and 4.

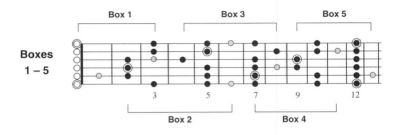

Once again, the pattern repeats above fret 12. All the notes are one octave higher than the corresponding box found lower on the fretboard.

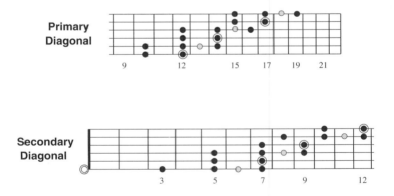

E blues, diagonals
The diagonal forms of the E blues scale are shown below, centered on box 1 (primary) and box 4 (secondary).

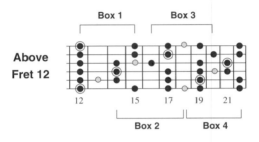

Fingering: For the primary diagonal, use ascending fingering (grouped in octaves) 1-3-1-1-2-3-1, 3-1-1-2-3-1, 3-1-1-2-3. Reverse this for descending. For the secondary diagonal, follow the same idea. The ascending fingering is (0)-1-1-2-3-1, 3-1-1-2-3-1, 3-1-1-2-3-1-3.

Other tonalities

Below are the full interconnected patterns for G blues, A blues, and C blues. Once again, notice the "anchor" chords. Also look for the diagonal forms sprouting in both directions from boxes 1 and 4.

G blues

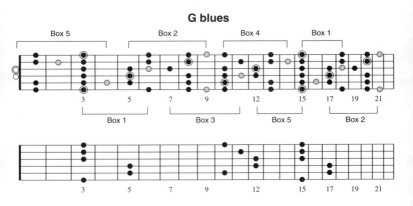

A blues

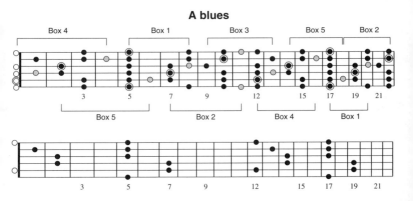

C blues

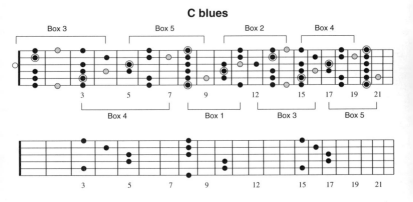

At this point, you have learned the blues scale in E, G, A, and C. For the remaining "in between" keys—F, F♯, G♯, B♭, B, C♯, D, and D♯—simply take the nearest key and slide up or down a fret or two, to place the root of the pattern on the correct pitch. (See page 63 for note names on the neck, if necessary.)

Major Pentatonic

The major pentatonic scale is a five-tone major scale common in rock, country, pop, blues-rock and other contemporary styles. Here are the notes, tones, and intervallic structure shown based on G.

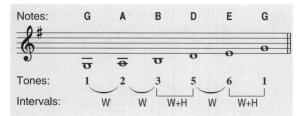

G major pentatonic, boxes 1 – 5

The box shapes of the major pentatonic scale are the same as those of the minor pentatonic scale, except that they lay against the root and "anchor" chords differently. Here, box 2 (not 1) is associated with the barre chord rooted on the sixth string. Look for these major barre chord shapes inside boxes 2 and 5.

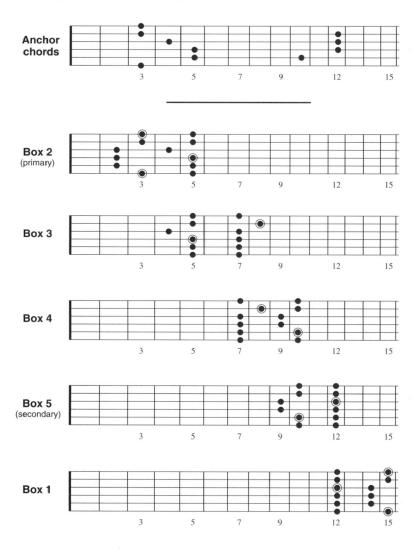

Fingering note: Use the same fingerings as for the minor pentatonic boxes on page 10.

Here are the five interconnected boxes for G major pentatonic. Play up and down each box, and shift from one to the next up and down the neck.

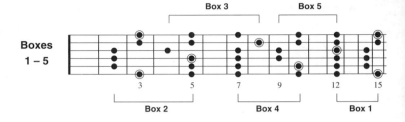

Next is the full neck for G major pentatonic. Of course, below box 2 there is a box 1 shape in open position. Although the low E string is in the scale, favor the G root at the third fret (start and end the box there). That way, your ear will hear G as the root, and hence, hear the scale as being a G major pentatonic rather than hearing the low E as the root. The boxes also continue in the same series above the fifteenth fret.

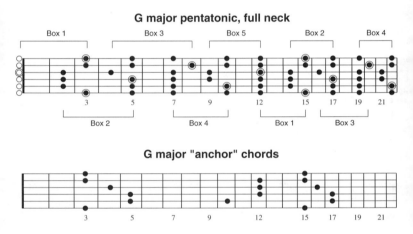

G major pentatonic, diagonals

The most common diagonal shapes used for G major pentatonic are shown below. The primary diagonal starts on the sixth string root, G—at the same position as the G barre chord at the third fret. The secondary diagonal contains the fifth string root, G—at the same position as the G barre chord at the tenth fret.

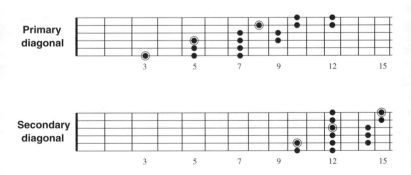

Other tonalities

Below are the full neck patterns for E, A, and C major pentatonic. Play the "anchor" chords, then all the patterns in each key, shifting from box to box, up and down the neck. Don't forget sequencing practice, too! Also, find and play the diagonal shapes (shown on the previous page in G) by shifting them to the proper positions for each key.

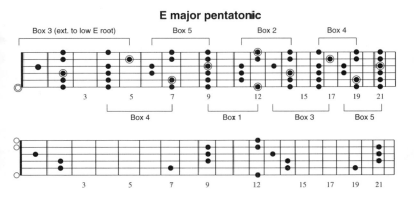

E major pentatonic

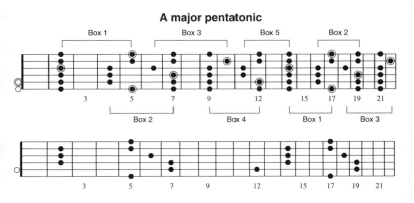

A major pentatonic

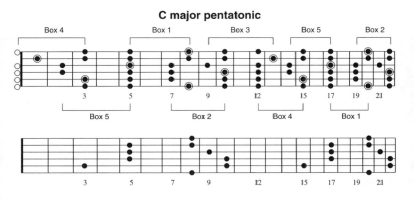

C major pentatonic

For the remaining keys, simply slide the nearest pattern up or down the neck. (See page 63 for note names on the neck.)

Relative major/minor tricks

Major and minor scales come in pairs. For every major scale, there is a corresponding minor scale that uses the exact same notes, but starts on a different root. We say these scales are *related*. Every major scale has a *relative* minor, and every minor scale has a *relative* major. For example, C major and A minor are related.

```
        C major
    ┌───────────┐
C D E F G A B C D E F G A B C
      └───────────┘
          A minor
```

In addition, C major pentatonic and A minor pentatonic are also relatives.

```
      C major pentatonic
    ┌─────────┐
  C D E G A C D E G A C
    └─────────┘
        A minor pentatonic
```

Another pair of relatives is G major and E minor. So as you would expect (and you may have already noticed), the G major pentatonic boxes on the previous page are identical to those shown on page 10 for E minor pentatonic. Again, only the roots (and anchor chords) are different.

One common way guitarists use this relative major/minor principle is to transform minor scales or licks into their major counterparts without having to learn any new patterns. You see, if you know the minor pentatonic scale, you can use the relative minor patterns to play the major pentatonic scale. For example, to play C major pentatonic, find the relative minor—A minor pentatonic. Now play A minor pentatonic over progressions in C major and your licks will give the sound of C major pentatonic.

In reality, your licks really are in C major pentatonic. (They only appear to use A minor pentatonic because you are familiar with seeing the patterns from a minor perspective.) The best situation is to learn the major pentatonic shapes anchored to their correct roots—in other words, seeing them truly as *major* pentatonics. Nevertheless, this bit of relative major/minor maneuvering can be useful and is something you should be aware of. Here is the rule:

> • To use minor patterns in a major key, apply the three-fret rule: *Drop three frets and use the relative minor pattern.*

To play G major, for example, drop three frets to E and use E minor. Here are a few relative major/minor pairs:

A minor	C major
E minor	G major
F♯ minor	A major
B minor	D major

> • The relative major is always the higher of the two; the minor is the lower of the two. The three-fret rule works in reverse, too. Raise any minor three frets and you'll have the relative major.

Minor Blues

The minor blues is an eight-tone scale created by combining the tones of a straight blues scale with those of natural minor (see page 26). Here are the notes, tones, and intervallic structure of the resulting hybrid scale beginning on A.

A minor blues, "boxes" 1 – 5

The patterns of the minor blues scale are not strictly "boxes" (they are more than two notes per string) but we will refer to them this way because this scale can be viewed as a minor pentatonic (or blues) with added color tones. Below, the A minor pentatonic boxes are shown in solid dots, with the added tones of A minor blues (2nd, b5th, b6th) shown in grey dots.

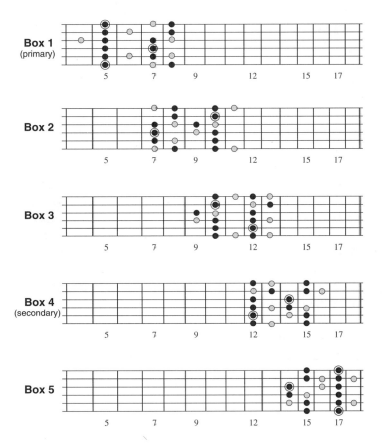

Fingering: Box 1 is in fifth position (stretch back a fret on string 3 then slide up immediately to play the remaining notes in fifth position). Box 2, in seventh position, utilizes a similar procedure (slide the fourth finger up a fret on strings 1 and 6). Where boxes 3, 4, and 5 call for four notes on a string, play the first three as positional fingering, then slide your fourth finger up to catch the last note. Reverse this for descending.

Here are the five interconnected patterns on the neck. Play up and down each pattern, shifting from one to the next until you can play it from memory. To help keep things straight, use the minor pentatonic shapes that you already know as a "skeletal" framework, upon which the extra notes of the minor blues can be seen to "hang."

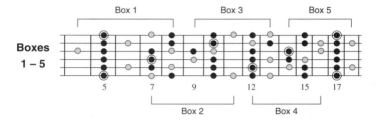

Now, try the full neck. Because of how the patterns lay together, one note appears doubled in bracketed boxes 4 and 1. Following the directions in parentheses will yield the same shapes as on the previous page.

A minor blues

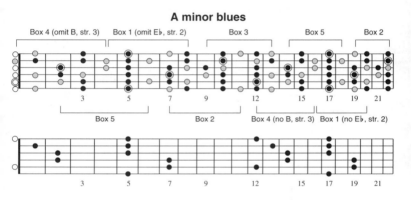

Other tonalities

Below, the minor blues scale is also shown in E and C. To play the scale in tonalities not shown here, simply shift the entire sequence of boxes up or down the fretboard. (See page 63 for note names on the neck.)

E minor blues

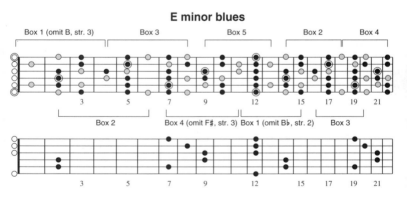

C minor blues

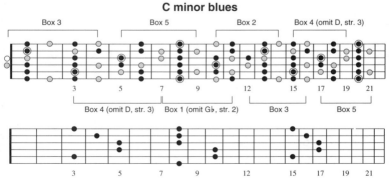

Major Blues

The major blues scale is a nine-tone scale created by combining the straight blues scale with the major tones of the Mixolydian mode (see page 42). Here are the notes, tones, and intervallic structure of this interesting hybrid scale shown based on A.

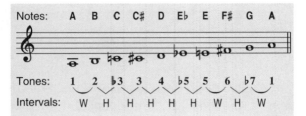

A major blues, "boxes" 1 – 5

Once again, the patterns of the minor blues scale are not strictly "boxes" (they are more than two notes per string), but we will refer to them this way because this scale can be viewed as a minor pentatonic (or blues) scale with added color tones. Below, the A minor pentatonic boxes are shown in solid dots, with the added tones of A major blues (2nd, 3rd, ♭5th, 6th) shown in grey dots.

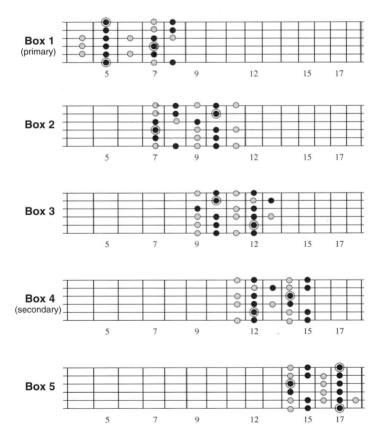

Fingering: Box 1 utilizes the *fifth* and *fourth positions* (where five notes occur, slide with the first or fourth finger). Box 2 is in *seventh position* (slide with the fourth finger for the extra note). Boxes 3, 4, and 5 are similar—slide with your fourth finger to catch the extra (fifth) fret.

Here are the five interconnected patterns on the neck. Play up and down each pattern, shifting from one to the next until you can play it from memory. To help keep things straight, use the minor pentatonic shapes that you already know as a "skeletal" framework, upon which the extra notes of the major blues "hang."

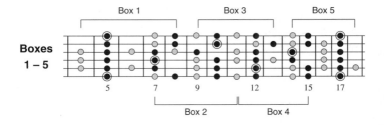

Next try the full neck. Use the A major anchor chords in boxes 1 and 4, below, to help locate positions more easily. Relating the scale to its anchor chords will also help you transpose it into other keys more readily.

A major blues

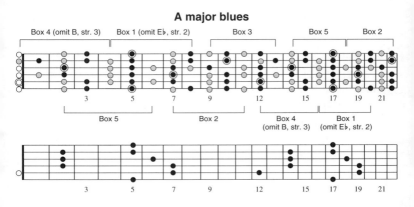

Other tonalities
Below, the major blues scale is also shown in E and C. To play the scale in tonalities not shown here, simply shift the entire sequence of boxes up or down the fretboard. (See page 63 for note names on the neck.)

E major blues

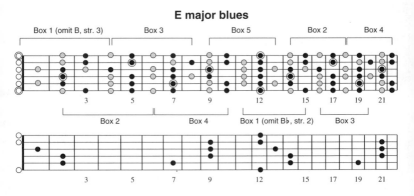

C major blues

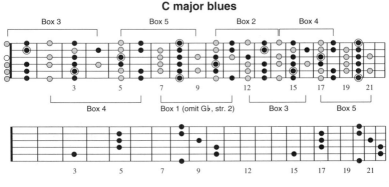

PART II

Natural Minor

The natural minor scale is the counterpart to the major scale—often considered its polar "opposite." This dark, sad-sounding scale is at home in metal, rock, pop, and folk styles. It is a seven-tone (diatonic) scale with a minor 3rd, minor 6th, and minor 7th. The notes, tones, and intervallic structure are shown below, based on E.

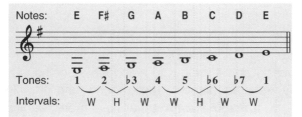

E natural minor, patterns 1 – 5

The natural minor scale has five different "positional" patterns on the neck. These contain and correspond to the minor pentatonic boxes (page 10). This makes learning the natural minor scale somewhat easier because you are just adding on to patterns previously learned. Below, the pentatonic boxes are shown in solid dots with added tones 2 and ♭6 shown in grey dots. Taken together, they form the full diatonic natural minor scale.

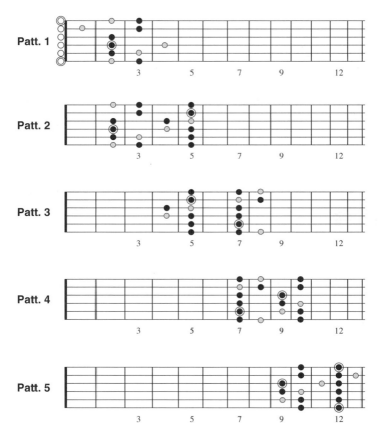

Fingering: Pattern 1 is in *open* (first) *position*. Pattern 2 is in *second position*. Pattern 3 is in *fifth position* (fourth for strings 3 and 4). Pattern 4 is in *seventh position*. Pattern 5 is in *ninth position* (tenth for strings 1 and 2).

Here is the entire neck for E natural minor. The "omit B, string 3" reference on lower pattern 1 tells you that one note which is unavoidably included in the bracketed area should be skipped. The higher pattern 1 begins at the eleventh fret, and so, does not need this indication.

• Pause the scale from time to time and play the Em anchor chords. This way, your ear will be sure to hear E as the root.

E natural minor

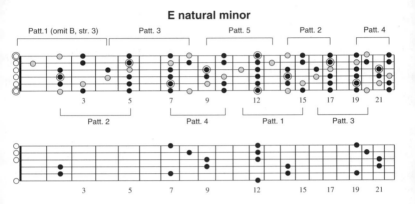

Other tonalities

Below are full neck patterns for A minor and C minor, along with the appropriate "anchor" chords. Play the chords and patterns for each tonality.

A natural minor

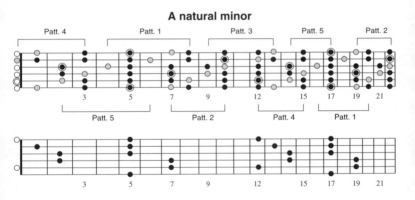

C natural minor

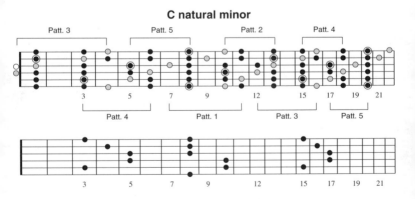

For other keys, simply slide the nearest pattern up or down the neck, placing the circled root locations at the appropriate fret. (See page 63 for note names on the neck, if necessary.)

E natural minor, three notes per string

For faster scale runs, three-note-per-string scale patterns are useful. There are seven different three-note-per-string patterns—one beginning on each tone of the scale. (Pattern 1 is shown at the octave position, below, as well.) These are excellent patterns for sequencing practice, and are very effective for building up your speed and picking technique.

- Consistent alternate picking is recommended, beginning with a downstroke. For example, when playing any of these patterns, string 6 will always be 'down-up-down' followed by 'up-down-up' on string 5. Repeat this approach on strings 4 and 3, then again on strings 2 and 1.

E natural minor

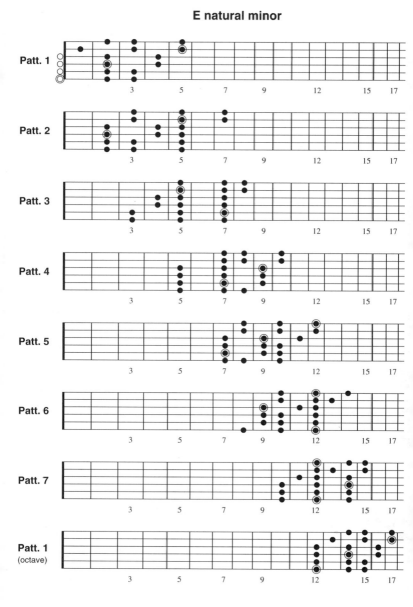

Fingering: When the notes span five frets on a string, use fingering 1–2–4 (or 1–3–4). Also, allow your position to change fluidly as needed through each pattern. For example, pattern 3 begins in third position (strings 5 and 6), changes to fourth position (strings 3 and 4), and changes again to fifth position (strings 1 and 2).

Other tonalities, three notes per string

Below are the three-note-per-string patterns for A and C natural minor. In each case, pattern 1 begins on the root on the sixth string, and the sequence of the patterns remains the same.

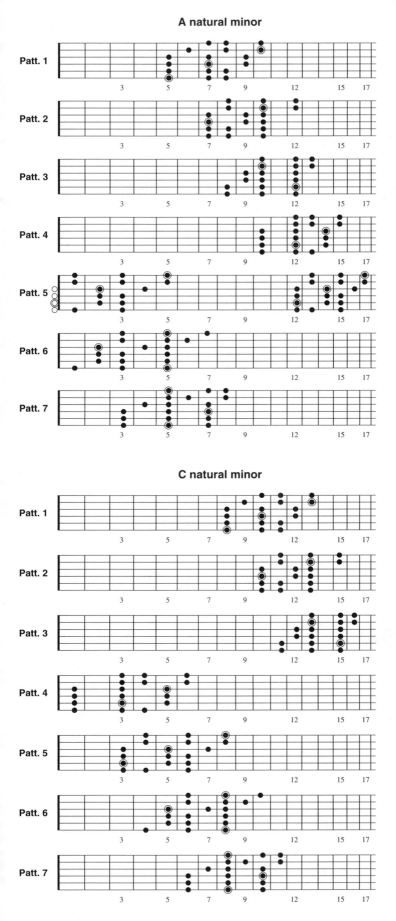

A natural minor

Patt. 1

Patt. 2

Patt. 3

Patt. 4

Patt. 5

Patt. 6

Patt. 7

C natural minor

Patt. 1

Patt. 2

Patt. 3

Patt. 4

Patt. 5

Patt. 6

Patt. 7

For other keys, simply slide the patterns up or down the neck. (See page 63 for note names on the neck.)

Major

The major scale is fundamental to Western music and appears in a variety of styles including pop, jazz, folk, and to a lesser extent, rock. It is bright and happy-sounding. Here are the notes, tones, and intervallic structure of this seven-tone (diatonic) scale, based on G.

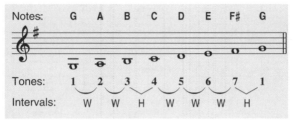

G major, patterns 1 – 5

The major scale has five distinct "positional" patterns on the neck. Since the major scale contains all the tones of major pentatonic (page 18), the pentatonic boxes appear within these major patterns. This makes learning the major scale somewhat easier because you are simply adding to patterns previously learned. Below, the major pentatonic boxes are shown in solid dots with added tones 4 and 7 shown in grey dots. Taken together, they form the diatonic major scale.

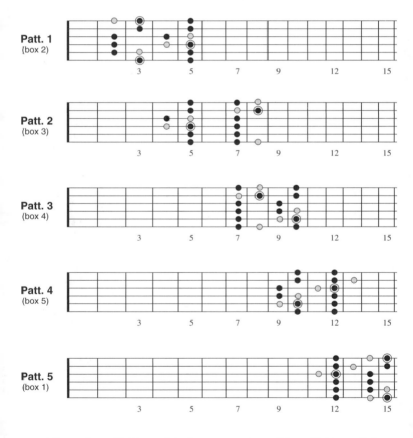

Fingering: Pattern 1 is in *second position*. Pattern 2 is in *fifth position* (*fourth* on strings 3 and 4). Pattern 3 is in *seventh position*. Pattern 4 is in *ninth position* (*tenth* on strings 1 and 2). Pattern 5 is in *twelfth position* (*eleventh* on string 3).

30

The astute guitarist will recognize that these patterns are the same as E minor (page 26). Only the roots and anchor chords are different—but this is a critical difference which changes how the ear hears the scale.

It is therefore wise to practice G major as its own set of patterns, to see it properly "attached" to its major anchors. Since you are familiar with the shapes already, learning them as G major should go quickly!

> • Pause the scale now and then to play the G chords. This way, your ear will be sure to hear G as the root. Also, try shifting between playing just the solid pentatonic dots and the full diatonic patterns. This makes for a great exercise!

G major

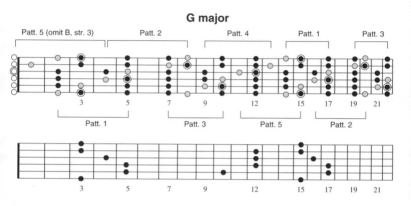

Other tonalities

Below are full neck patterns for E and C major, along with the appropriate "anchor" chords. Play the chords and patterns for each tonality.

E major

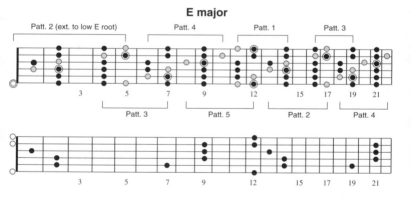

C major

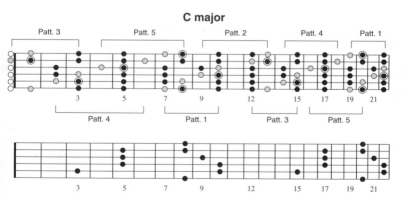

For other keys, simply slide the nearest pattern up or down the neck. (See page 63 for note names on the neck, if necessary.)

G major, three notes per string

For faster scale runs, three-note-per-string scale patterns are useful. There are seven different three-note-per-string patterns—one beginning on each tone of the scale. Once again, these are the same patterns you learned as E natural minor (page 28). Here, however, we will anchor them to G roots and G major chords.

> • Consistent alternate picking is recommended, beginning with a downstroke. For example, when playing any of these patterns, string 6 will always be 'down-up-down' followed by 'up-down-up' on string 5. Repeat this approach on strings 4 and 3, then again on strings 2 and 1.

G major

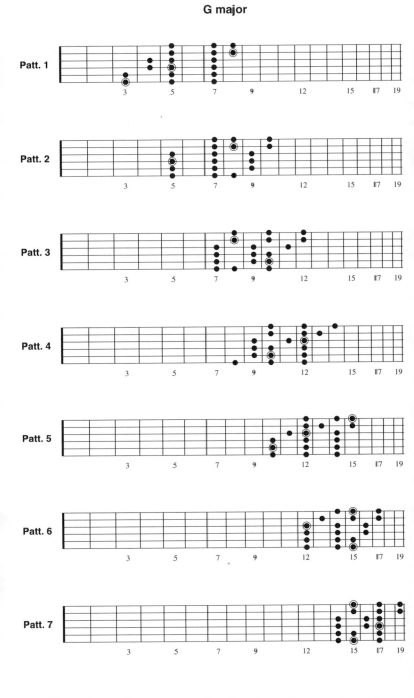

Fingering: Same as natural minor three-note-per-string patterns (see page 28).

Other tonalities, three notes per string

Below are the three-note-per-string patterns for E and C major. Number 1 begins on the root on string 6 and the sequence of the patterns always remains the same.

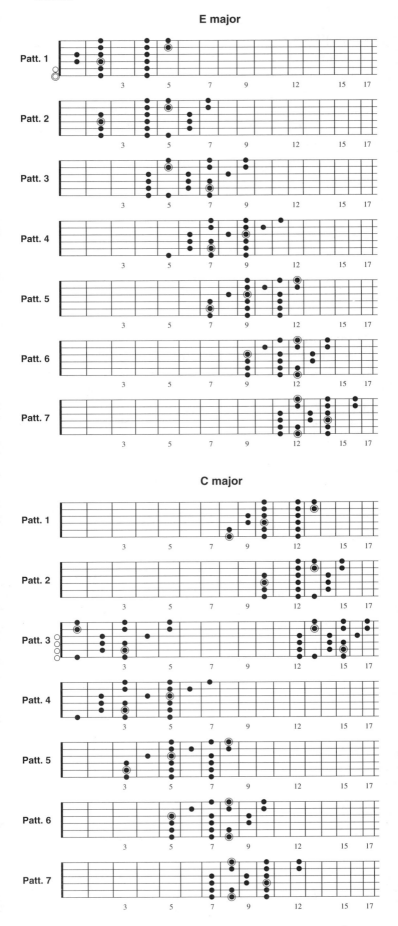

E major

C major

For other keys, simply slide the patterns up or down the neck. (See page 63 for note names on the neck.)

Creating Modes

Modes are created when the root note of a "parent" scale is displaced. For example, let's take C major. Played from C to C, this is simply the C major scale itself. In modal terms, this is the *first mode* of C major. Next use the same notes, but this time play them from D to D—making the second note of the scale (D) to be the root—and you have the *second mode* of C major. Play from E to E and you have the *third mode* of C major, and so on. There are seven different notes in the scale, so there are a total of seven different modes.

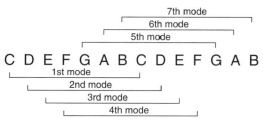

Modal names

The seven different modes of the major scale are named with the following Greek names. Notice how each mode of C major is completely contained within the same overall C major pattern 1.

> • The Ionian mode is the modal name for the major scale itself. The Aeolian mode is the modal name for the natural minor scale.

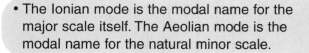

1	C Ionian (major)
2	D Dorian
3	E Phrygian
4	F Lydian
5	G Mixolydian
6	A Aeolian (nat. minor)
7	B Locrian

Each mode may be viewed as a scale in its own right. Below are the modes derived from the G major parent scale, shown in full, two-octave shapes.

• Look for a G major barre chord within the G Ionian pattern, an A minor chord within the A Dorian pattern, a B minor chord within the B Phrygian pattern, a C major chord within the C Lydian pattern, a D major chord within the D Mixolydian pattern, an E minor chord within the E Aeolian patter, and an F♯ diminished chord within the F♯ Locrian pattern.

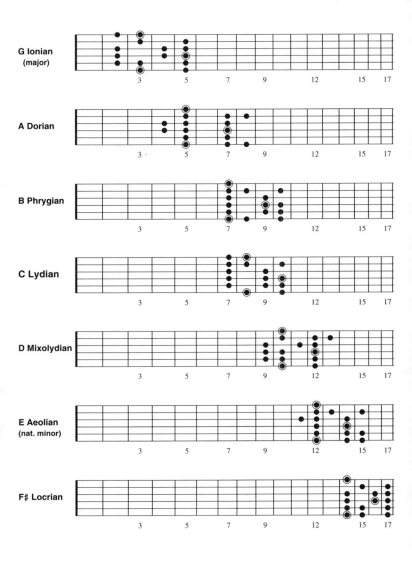

All modes derived from any parent scale (a modal family) are said to be *related*—this means that they share the same notes. It is important to realize that it is the placement of the roots which cause each pattern to be a particular mode. Delete the root information above and *all* of the patterns can be G major. They also could *all* be A Dorian, B Phrygian, C Lydian, D Mixolydian, E Aeolian, or F♯ Locrian.

On the following pages, the modes (other than Ionian and Aeolian) are each covered as scales in their own right, over the entire fretboard.

Dorian

The Dorian mode is a natural minor scale with a raised (major) sixth step, making it a distinctly minor type of scale with a moment of brightness. It is common in rock and pop styles. The notes, tones, and intervallic structure are shown below, based on E.

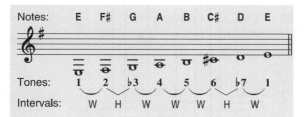

E Dorian, patterns 1 – 5

The Dorian mode has five different "positional" patterns on the neck. These contain and correspond to the minor pentatonic boxes (page 10). Below, the pentatonic boxes are shown in solid dots with added tones 2 and 6 shown in grey dots. Taken together, they form the full diatonic Dorian mode.

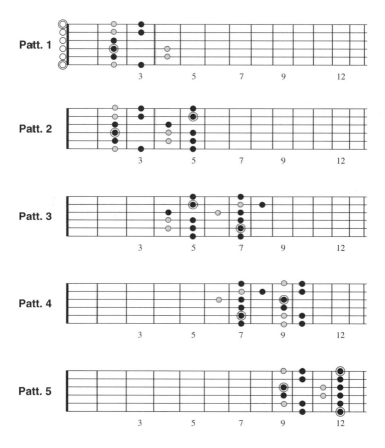

Fingering: Pattern 1 is in *open* (first) *position*. Pattern 2 is in *second position*. Pattern 3 is in *fourth position* (fifth for strings 1 and 2). Pattern 4 is in *seventh position* (stretch back a fret on string 3). Pattern 5 is in *ninth position* (tenth for strings 1 and 2).

The astute guitarist may notice that E Dorian uses the patterns of D major/B minor (but with roots on E). Nevertheless, it is best to learn each mode as a scale in its own right, with its parallel, "superimposed" pentatonic and anchor chords. This will also allow for quick and easy parallel modality changes—for example, changing between E natural minor and E Dorian "on the fly" during a guitar solo—using a relative pattern will not.

E Dorian

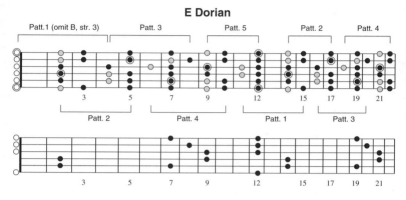

Other Tonalities
Here is the A Dorian mode along with the associated Am anchor chords. Shift it into other keys as well.

A Dorian

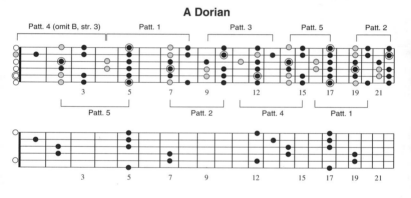

Three notes per string
You should already know the diatonic three-note-per-string patterns and sequence (pages 28 and 32), so all you really need here is the correct starting point. The shape shown on page 32 as "pattern 2" becomes pattern 1 for Dorian. Shift it to start on the sixth string root. In this case, to play G Dorian, we'll start with this pattern on G at the third fret and continue from there.

G Dorian

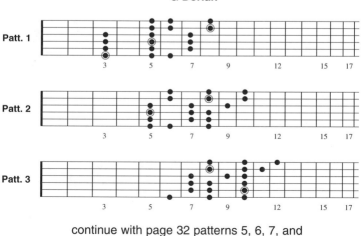

continue with page 32 patterns 5, 6, 7, and 1 as 4, 5, 6, and 7 (down two frets)...

Phrygian

The Phrygian mode is a natural minor scale with a flatted (minor) second step, which adds a distinctly Spanish flavor. It is common in metal and alternative rock. The notes, tones, and intervallic structure are shown below, based on E.

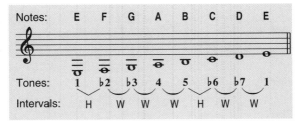

E Phrygian, patterns 1 – 5
The five positional patterns of the Phrygian mode are shown below. The pentatonic boxes contained within the patterns are shown in solid dots with added tones ♭2 and ♭6 shown in grey dots. Taken together, they form the full diatonic Phrygian mode.

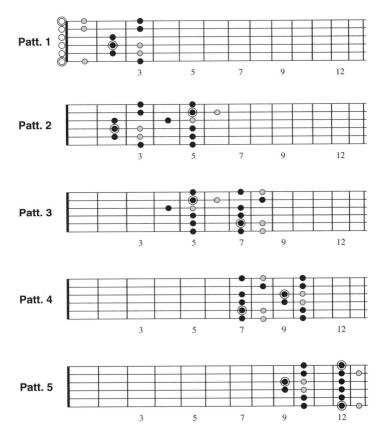

Fingering: Pattern 1 is in *open* (first) *position*. Pattern 2 is in *second position* (third for strings 1 and 2). Pattern 3 is in *fifth position* (stretch back a fret on string 3). Pattern 4 is in *seventh position*. Pattern 5 is in *tenth position* (ninth for strings 3 and 4).

The astute guitarist may notice that E Phrygian uses the patterns of C major/A minor (but with roots on E). Nevertheless, it is best to learn each mode as a scale in its own right, with its parallel, "superimposed" pentatonic and anchor chords. This will also allow for quick and easy parallel modality changes—for example, changing between E natural minor and E Phrygian "on the fly" during a guitar solo—using a relative pattern will not.

E Phrygian

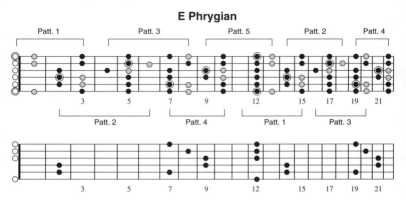

Other Tonalities
Here is the A Phrygian mode along with Am anchor chords. Shift this into other keys as well.

A Phrygian

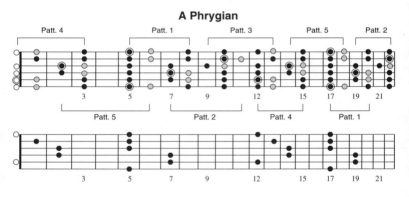

Three notes per string
You should already know the diatonic three-note-per-string patterns and sequence (pages 28 and 32), so all you really need here is the correct starting point. The shape shown on page 32 as "pattern 3" becomes pattern 1 for Phrygian. Shift it to the sixth string root. In this case, to play G Phrygian, we'll start with this pattern on G at the third fret and continue from there.

G Phrygian

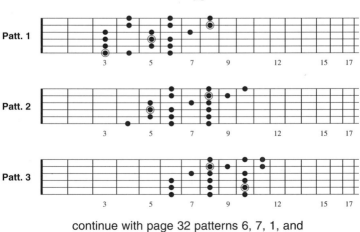

continue with page 32 patterns 6, 7, 1, and
2 as 4, 5, 6, and 7 (down four frets)...

Lydian

The Lydian mode is a major scale with a raised (augmented) fourth step, which gives it an odd, mysterious quality. The notes, tones, and intervallic structure are shown below, based on G.

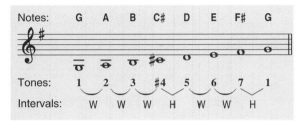

G Lydian, patterns 1 – 5

The Lydian mode has five different "positional" patterns on the neck. These contain and correspond to the major pentatonic boxes (page 18). Below, the pentatonic boxes are shown in solid dots with added tones #4 and 7 shown in grey dots. Taken together, they form the full diatonic Lydian mode.

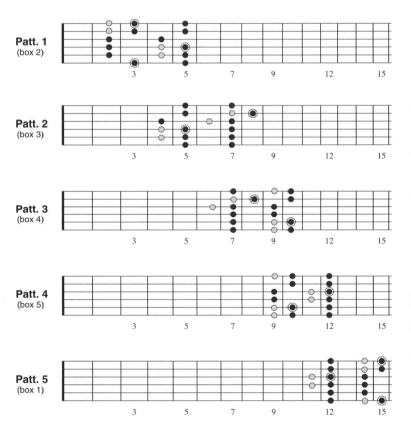

Fingering: Pattern 1 is in *second position*. Pattern 2 is in *fourth position* (fifth for strings 1 and 2). Pattern 3 is in *seventh position* (stretch back a fret for string 3). Pattern 4 is in *ninth position*. Pattern 5 is in *twelfth position* (eleventh for strings 3 and 4).

The astute guitarist may notice that G Lydian uses the patterns of D major/B minor (as well as those of E Dorian shown on page 36), simply with displaced roots. However, it is best to learn each mode as a scale in its own right, with its "superimposed" pentatonic and proper anchor chords. This will also allow for quick and easy parallel modality changes "on the fly" during a guitar solo—using a relative pattern will not.

G Lydian

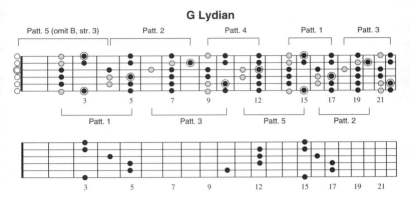

Other Tonalities

Here is the C Lydian mode with its associated anchor chords. Shift into other keys as well.

C Lydian

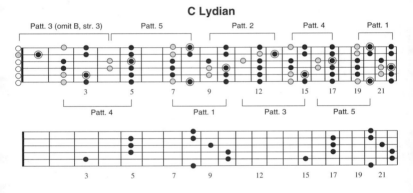

Three notes per string

You should already know the diatonic three-note-per-string patterns and sequence (pages 28 and 32), so all you really need here is the correct starting point. The shape shown on page 32 as "pattern 4" becomes pattern 1 for Lydian. Shift it to the sixth string root. In this case, to play E Lydian, we'll start with this pattern on open E and continue from there.

E Lydian

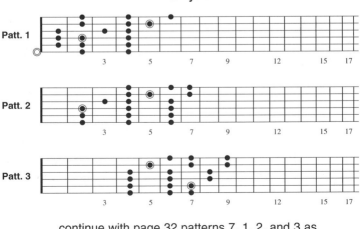

continue with page 32 patterns 7, 1, 2, and 3 as 4, 5, 6, and 7 (down eight frets, or up four)...

Mixolydian

The Mixolydian mode is a major scale with a flatted (minor) seventh step. This is common in rock and pop styles, where it is often used as a major-sounding mode in place of the major scale. It contains the tones of the dominant seventh chord. The notes, tones, and intervallic structure are shown below, based on G.

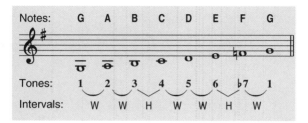

G Mixolydian, patterns 1 – 5

The Mixolydian mode has five different "positional" patterns on the neck. These contain and correspond to the major pentatonic boxes (page 18). Below, the pentatonic boxes are shown in solid dots with added tones 4 and ♭7 shown in grey dots. Taken together, they form the full diatonic Mixolydian mode.

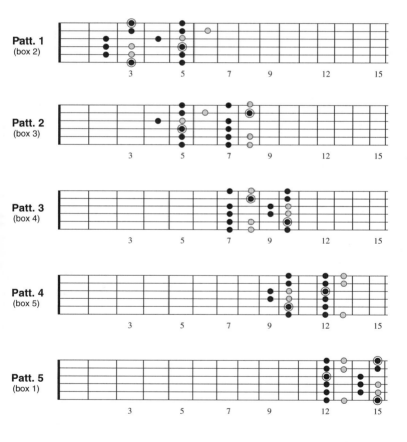

Fingering: Pattern 1 is in *second position* (third for strings 1 and 2). Pattern 2 is in *fifth position* (stretch back a fret for string 3). Pattern 3 is in *seventh position*. Pattern 4 is in *tenth position* (ninth for strings 3 and 4). Pattern 5 is in *twelfth position*.

The astute guitarist may notice that G Mixolydian uses the patterns of C major/A minor, simply with displaced roots. However, it is best to learn each mode as a scale in its own right, with its "superimposed" pentatonic and proper anchor chords. This will also allow for quick and easy parallel modality changes "on the fly" during a guitar solo—using a relative pattern will not.

G Mixolydian

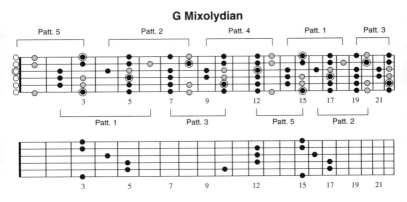

Other Tonalities
Here is the C Mixolydian mode with its associated anchor chords. Shift into other keys as well.

C Mixolydian

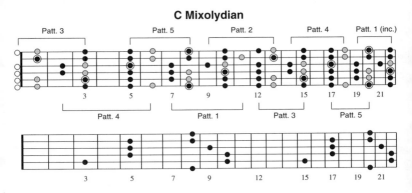

Three notes per string
You should already know the diatonic three-note-per-string patterns and sequence (pages 28 and 32), so all you really need here is the correct starting point. The shape shown on page 32 as "pattern 5" becomes pattern 1 for Mixolydian. Shift it to the sixth string root. In this case, to play E Mixolydian, start with this pattern on open E and continue from there.

E Mixolydian

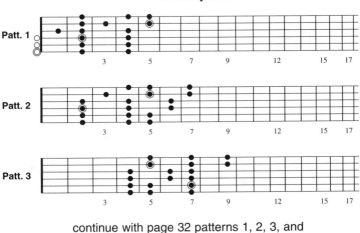

continue with page 32 patterns 1, 2, 3, and 4 as 4, 5, 6, and 7 (up two frets)...

Locrian

The Locrian mode is like the Phrygian mode with a flatted (diminished) fifth step. It is common in the heaviest forms of modern metal. It contains the tones of the diminished (and minor seven flat five) chord. The notes, tones, and intervallic structure are shown below, based on E.

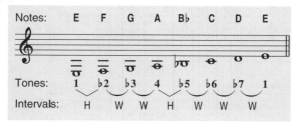

E Locrian, patterns 1 – 5
The five positional patterns of the Locrian mode are shown below. The pentatonic boxes must be altered to form a "pentatonic ♭5" scale to conform to the Locrian mode's diminished fifths. This is shown in solid dots with added tones ♭2 and ♭6 shown in grey dots. Taken together, they form the full diatonic Locrian mode.

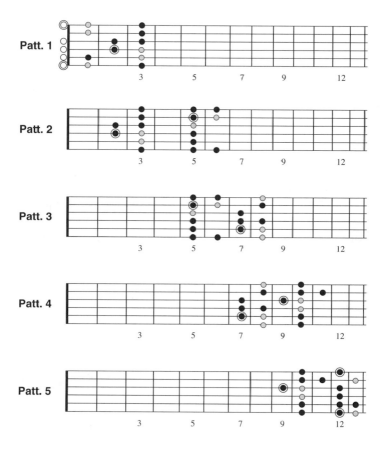

Fingering: Pattern 1 is in *open* (first) *position*. Pattern 2 is in *third position* (second for strings 3 and 4). Pattern 3 is in *fifth position*. Pattern 4 is in *seventh position* (eighth for strings 1 and 2). Pattern 5 is in *tenth position* (stretch back a fret for string 3).

The astute guitarist may notice that E Locrian uses the patterns of F major/D minor (but with roots on E). Nevertheless, it is best to learn each mode as a scale in its own right, with the "superimposed" pentatonic and anchor chords.

• The anchor chords shown are m7♭5 types.

E Locrian

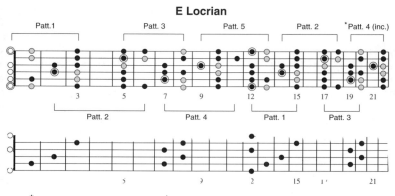

*Pattern is incomplete; include B♭ either on string 2, fret 23, or string 1, fret 18.

Other tonalities
Here is the A Locrian mode along with Am anchor chords. Shift this into other keys as well.

A Locrian

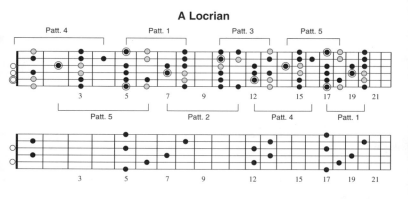

Three notes per string
You should already know the diatonic three-note-per-string patterns and sequence (pages 28 and 32), so all you really need here is the correct starting point. The shape shown on page 32 as "pattern 7" becomes pattern 1 for Locrian. Shift it to the sixth string root. In this case, to play G Locrian, start with this pattern on G at the third fret and continue from there.

G Locrian

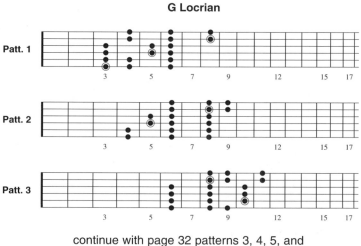

continue with page 32 patterns 3, 4, 5, and 6 as 4, 5, 6, and 7 (up one fret)...

PART III

Harmonic Minor

The harmonic minor scale is a natural minor with a raised (major) seventh step. This creates an exotic-sounding three-fret interval flanked by half steps. It may also be used create a strong minor resolution, and is common in the neo-classical style. The notes, tones, and intervallic structure are shown below on E.

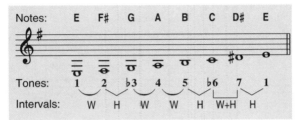

Notes:	E	F#	G	A	B	C	D#	E
Tones:	1	2	b3	4	5	b6	7	1
Intervals:		W	H	W	W	H	W+H	H

E harmonic minor, patterns 1 – 5

The harmonic minor scale can be played in five different "positional" patterns on the neck. The easiest way to learn them is to take natural minor and raise each 7th step one fret (so it is found a half step below each root). Of course, this approach assumes you already know the natural minor. If not, review the patterns on page 26. The major 7ths are shown in grey.

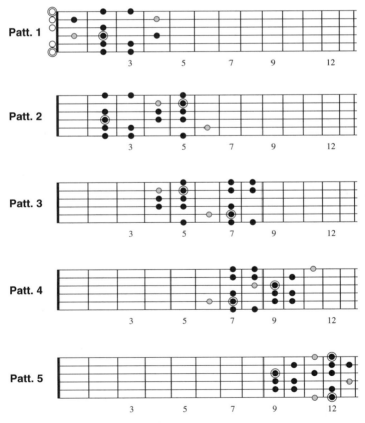

Fingering: Pattern 1 is in *open* (first) *position*. Pattern 2 is in *second position* (stretch fourth finger up on string 5). Pattern 3 is in *fifth* and *fourth positions*. Pattern 4 starts in *sixth position* and shifts up to seventh position on string 5. Pattern 5 is in *ninth position* (tenth for strings 1 and 2).

Here is the entire neck for E harmonic minor. Because of how the patterns connect together, the B note appears doubled in lower pattern 1. Follow the directions in parenthesis to avoid playing this note twice. The higher pattern 1 begins at the eleventh fret, and so avoids this situation.

> • Pause the scale from time to time and play the Em anchor chords to hear E as the root.

E harmonic minor

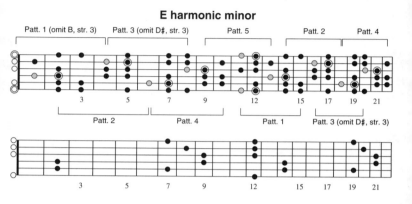

Other tonalities
Below are full neck patterns for A and C harmonic minor, along with the anchor chords. Play the patterns for each tonality. Then shift into other keys.

A harmonic minor

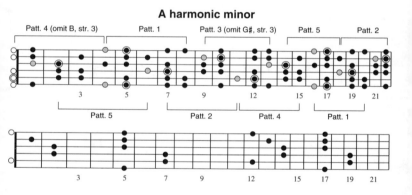

C harmonic minor

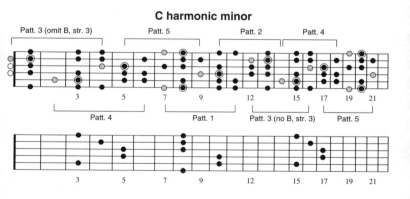

For other keys, simply slide the nearest pattern up or down the neck. (See page 63 for note names on the neck, if necessary.)

E harmonic minor, three notes per string

For faster scale runs, three-note-per-string scale patterns are useful. There are seven different three-note-per-string patterns—one beginning on each tone of the scale. (Pattern 1 is also shown at the octave position, below.)

> • Consistent alternate picking is recommended, beginning with a downstroke. For example, when playing any of these patterns, string 6 will always be 'down-up-down' followed by 'up-down-up' on string 5. Repeat this approach on strings 4 and 3, then again on strings 2 and 1.

E harmonic minor

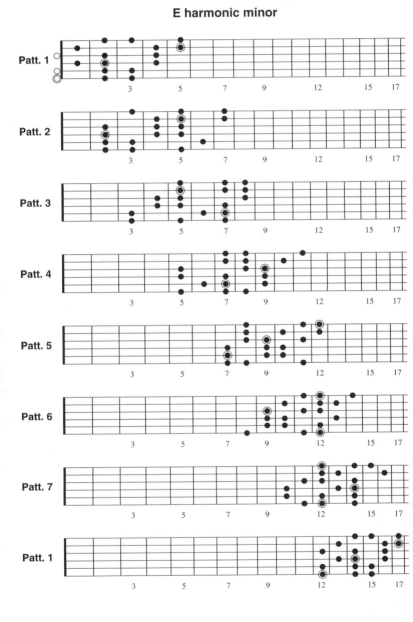

Fingering: Allow your position to change fluidly through each pattern. For example, pattern 2 begins in second position, changes to fourth position (string 2), and stretches back a fret on string 1. When spanning five frets with whole steps (as in pattern 3, string 6), use fingering 1–2–4. When spanning five frets with a minor third and half step (as in pattern 3, string 5), use fingering 1–3–4.

Other tonalities, three notes per string

Below are the three-note-per-string patterns for A and C harmonic minor. In each case, pattern 1 begins on the root on the sixth string, and the sequence of the patterns remains the same as on the previous page.

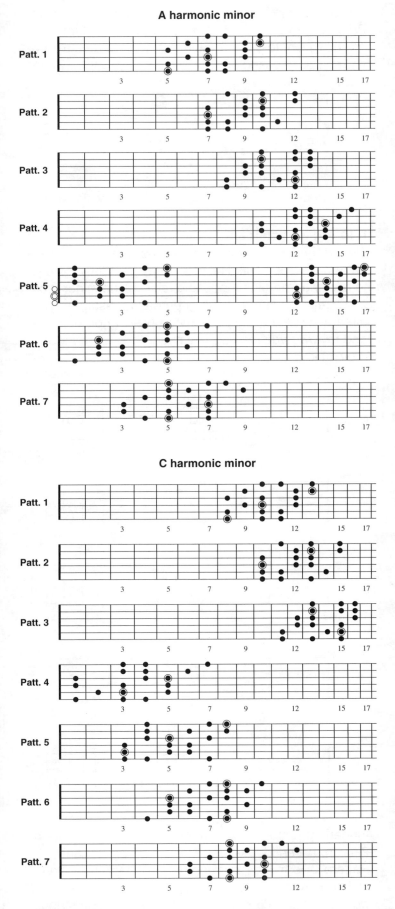

A harmonic minor

C harmonic minor

For other keys, simply slide the patterns up or down the neck. (See page 63 for note names on the neck.)

Phrygian-Dominant

The Phrygian-dominant scale is a Phrygian mode with a raised (major) 3rd. This is also called the Spanish Phrygian, major Phrygian, or Spanish Flamenco scale. The notes, tones, and intervallic structure are shown below based on E.

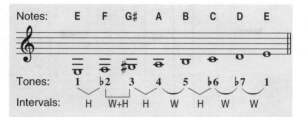

E Phrygian-dominant, patterns 1 – 5

The Phrygian-dominant scale has five "positional" patterns on the neck. The easiest way to learn them is to take the Phrygian mode and raise all the minor 3rds one fret. Of course, this approach assumes you already know the Phrygian mode well. If not, go back and review page 38 first. The major 3rds are shown in grey, below.

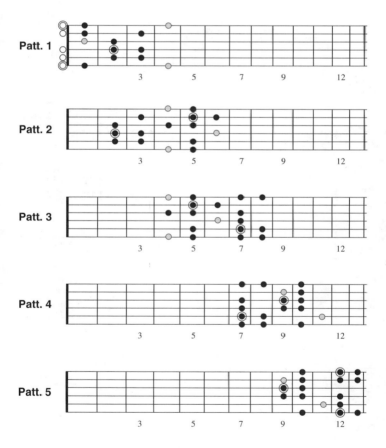

Fingering: Pattern 1 is in *open (first) position*. Pattern 2 is in *second position* (*third* on strings 1 and 2). Pattern 3 is in *fifth position* (stretch back a fret and slide up on strings 1, 3, and 6). Pattern 4 is in *seventh position*. Pattern 5 is in *tenth position* (*ninth* on strings 3 and 4, slide back up to tenth on string 2).

Whole Tone

The whole tone scale is another atonal scale with equidistant tones. This time, each note is a whole step apart, and there are six tones per octave. It gives an odd sort of "lost" quality. Below, the notes, tones, and intervallic structure are shown based on E.

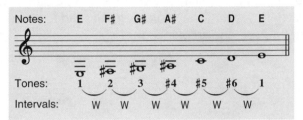

Notes:	E	F#	G#	A#	C	D	E
Tones:	1	2	3	#4	#5	#6	1
Intervals:	W	W	W	W	W	W	

Whole tone scale, positional

Again, any note can be made to be the root since all tones are equidistant. Therefore, there are only two different whole tone scales—one starting on any given note and a another one starting a half step higher (or lower). Below is the positional pattern beginning on G at the third fret. Notice how the pattern can be moved up two frets at a time and it is still the same scale, using exactly the same pattern.

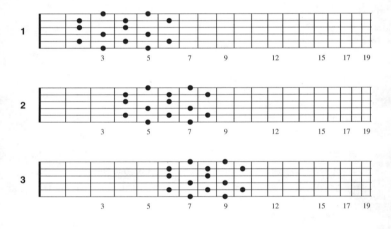

Whole tone scale, three notes per string

The three-note-per string whole-tone pattern is shown below. It may also be shifted up two frets at a time without changing the pattern or tonality. Use fingering 1–2–4 on each string.

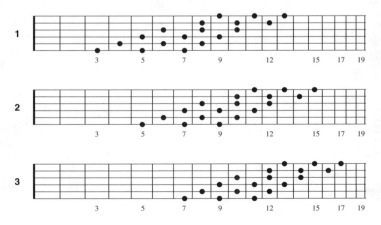

Diminished

The diminished scale comes in two varieties: the whole-half and half-whole. Both are atonal, with every second note spelling out a diminished 7th arpeggio.

Whole-half

The whole-half scale is a sequence of repeating whole and half steps. The notes, tones, and intervallic structure are shown below on E.

Below are positional and diagonal shapes for the G whole-half diminished scale. Similar to the idea in the whole tone scale, each can be shifted in increments of *three* frets without altering the pattern or tonality. Therefore, these effectively cover the entire neck.

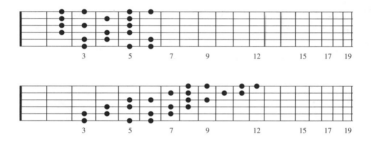

Half-whole

The half-whole scale simply reverses the pattern of half and whole steps. The notes, tones, and intervallic structure are shown below on E. (Every second note still spells the E diminished 7th arpeggio as above).

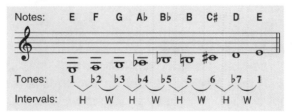

Below are positional and diagonal shapes for the G half-whole diminished scale. Again, each can be shifted in increments of *three frets* at a time without altering the pattern or tonality. Therefore, these effectively cover the entire neck.

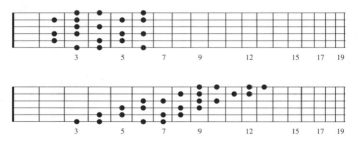

The astute guitarist will recognize that these patterns are the same as A harmonic minor, but with different roots and anchor chords. This is because the Phrygian-dominant scale happens to be a mode of harmonic minor (the fifth mode, to be precise).

> • Listen for the interesting mix of the bright major 3rds (in grey) against the other minor intervals. The anchord chords are E major.

E Phrygian-dominant

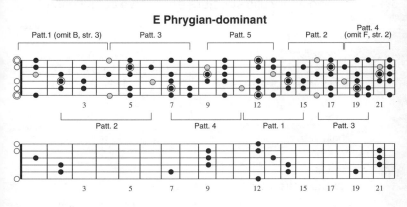

Other tonalities

Below the Phrygian-dominant scale is shown in A with the appropriate anchor chords. Shift the patterns to play in other tonalities as well.

A Phrygian-dominant

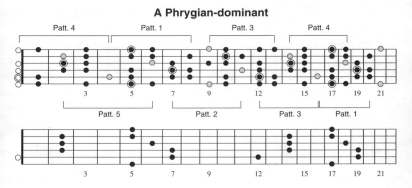

Three notes per string

Phrygian-dominant uses the same patterns and sequence as harmonic minor (page 48), but with different roots. The shape shown on page 48 as "pattern 5" becomes pattern 1 here. Shift it to begin on the sixth string root. In this case, to play G Phrygian-dominant, we'll start on G at the third fret.

G Phrygian-dominant

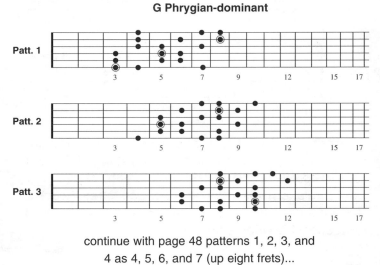

continue with page 48 patterns 1, 2, 3, and 4 as 4, 5, 6, and 7 (up eight frets)...

Jazz Melodic Minor

The jazz melodic minor scale is a natural minor with raised (major) 6th and 7th steps. This makes it the brightest-sounding minor scale—in fact, the top half of the scale is identical to the major scale. The notes, tones, and intervallic structure are shown below based on E.

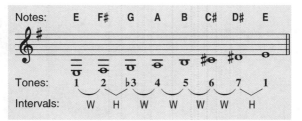

E jazz melodic minor, patterns 1 – 5
The jazz melodic minor scale (sometimes called simply "jazz minor") has five positional patterns on the neck. The easiest way to learn them is to take the major scale and drop all the 3rds one fret. Of course, this approach assumes you already know the major scale well. If not, it is recommended that you review page 30 first. The minor 3rds are shown in grey.

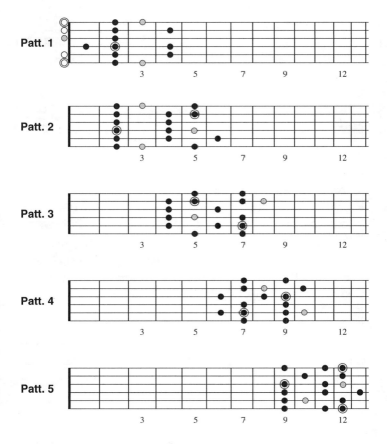

Fingering: Pattern 1 is in *open (first) position*. Pattern 2 is in *second position* (use 1–2–4 on string 5). Pattern 3 is in *fourth position* (slide up into fifth on strings 1 and 2). Pattern 4 is in *seventh position* (stretch back a fret on strings 3 and 5). Pattern 5 is in *ninth position* (fingering 1–2–4 on string 4).

Here is the full neck for E jazz minor. Omit the B note of string 3 in the lower bracketed pattern 1. The higher pattern 1 avoids this situation by including fret 11.

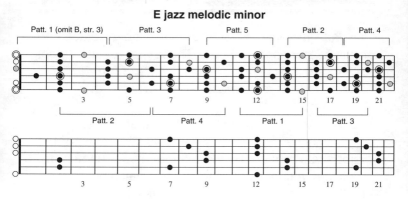

E jazz melodic minor

Other tonalities

Here is the A jazz minor scale along with the Am anchor chords. Shift into other keys, as well.

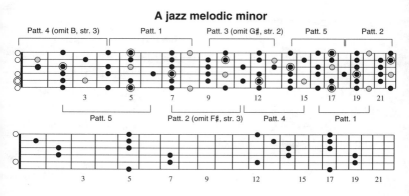

A jazz melodic minor

Three notes per string

Below, the jazz minor scale is shown in three-note-per-string patterns in G. Shift into other keys, as well.

G jazz melodic minor

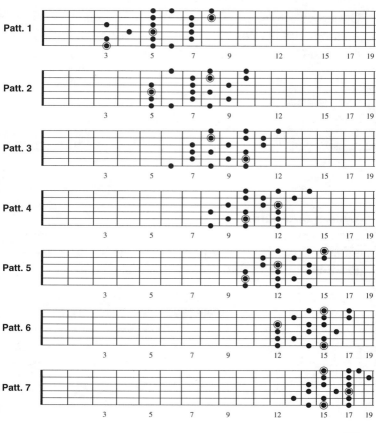

Modes of Jazz Minor

The jazz melodic minor scale may be displaced to create a series of modes. These are used almost exclusively in advanced jazz styles, and are relatively complex. That said, most guitarists will never have need to master these. Nevertheless, for the curious and the jazz-minded we will outline them here.

These modes are viewed as alterations of the major-scale modes, so the original modal names are employed along with descriptive tonal labels which identify the particular variation. Make sure you know all the major-scale modes very well before tackling these!

Each mode below is shown in its pattern 1, with its root on the sixth string.

Jazz melodic minor
This is the parent scale (and first mode). It doesn't have a special modal name—we just call it the jazz melodic minor scale. This example starts with A jazz melodic minor, which you already learned on the previous page, but here it is again (pattern 1). The notes are A–B–C–D–E–F♯–G♯, so the following modes will each begin on one of these notes.

A jazz melodic minor

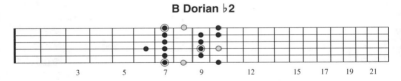

Dorian ♭2
Dorian ♭2 is the second mode of the jazz minor scale. As the name implies, this is simply a Dorian mode with a flatted (minor) 2nd tone. Below, the ♭2s are shown in grey.

B Dorian ♭2

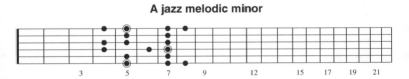

Lydian augmented
Lydian augmented is the third mode of the jazz minor scale. This is a Lydian mode with a raised (augmented) 5th. Below, the ♯5s are shown in grey.

C Lydian augmented

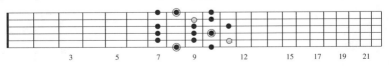

Lydian ♭7

Lydian ♭7 is the fourth mode of the jazz minor scale. This is a Lydian mode with a flat (minor) 7th. This structure is also known as the overtone scale. Below, the ♭7s are shown in grey.

D Lydian ♭7

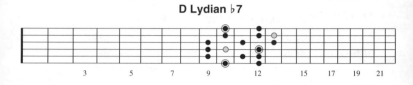

Mixolydian ♭13

Mixolydian ♭13 is the fifth mode of the jazz minor scale. This is a Mixolydian mode with a flat (minor) 6th. (The ♭6th is known as a ♭13th because extended jazz chords use this note generally in a higher octave. This name, then, has been retained even though the note in question does in fact appear in every octave of the scale.) This structure is also known as the Hindu scale. Below, the ♭6s/♭13s are shown in grey.

E Mixolydian ♭13

Locrian ♯2

Locrian ♯2 is the sixth mode of the jazz minor scale. This is a Locrian mode with a raised 2nd. Since Locrian, however, starts out with a flat (minor) 2nd, raising it simply brings it back up to a "normal" major 2nd. Below, the 2nds are shown in grey.

F♯ Locrian ♯2

Super Locrian (altered)

The super Locrian mode is the seventh mode of the jazz minor scale. It is also known as the "altered scale." It consists of a Locrian mode with a flat 4th. In this case, every tone other than the root is flatted! Below, the 4ths are shown in grey.

G♯ super Locrian (or altered)

Remember: As with the previous modes (page 34), all the modes here share the same notes. Delete the root information and all the patterns fit A jazz minor as well as B Dorian ♭2, C Lydian augmented, etc. To play in other keys, shift the patterns up or down the neck as appropriate.

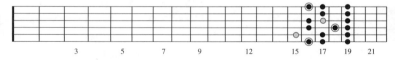

55

The chromatic scale simply uses every half step. So it has twelve tones per octave. It is rarely used in its entirety. Rather, small portions of the scale may be used within another tonality to "smooth out" a line and add some passing chromatic interest.

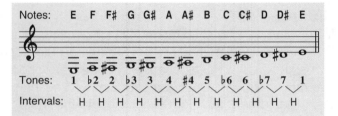

Chromatic scale, positional (all tonalities)

Since all tones are equidistant, there is no structure that the ear can "latch on" to and regard as the root. We say it is an *atonal* scale. Any note can be made to be the root, so there is really only one chromatic scale. (Or, to say it another way, every chromatic scale is a mode of every other chromatic scale.) The same "positional" pattern, then, may be played at any fret. The only difference is when open strings are involved. Below, it is shown starting on the low E.

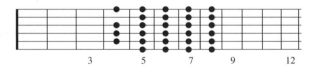

Here it is played from A to A, in fifth/fourth position. Slide either your first or fourth finger to play five notes per string.

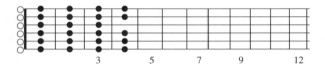

Chromatic scale, up a single string

Below, the chromatic scale is played from A to A, up and down on a single string. Use the fingering 0–1–2–3–4, then shift up to fifth position and use 1–2–3–4, then shift up again to ninth position for another 1–2–3–4. Reverse the sequence to come back down.

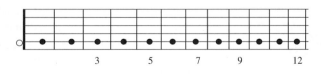

Whole Tone

The whole tone scale is another atonal scale with equidistant tones. This time, each note is a whole step apart, and there are six tones per octave. It gives an odd sort of "lost" quality. Below, the notes, tones, and intervallic structure are shown based on E.

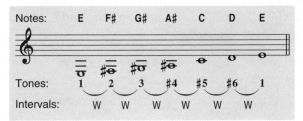

Whole tone scale, positional

Again, any note can be made to be the root since all tones are equidistant. Therefore, there are only two different whole tone scales—one starting on any given note and a another one starting a half step higher (or lower). Below is the positional pattern beginning on G at the third fret. Notice how the pattern can be moved up two frets at a time and it is still the same scale, using exactly the same pattern.

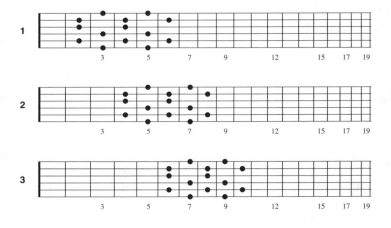

Whole tone scale, three notes per string

The three-note-per string whole-tone pattern is shown below. It may also be shifted up two frets at a time without changing the pattern or tonality. Use fingering 1–2–4 on each string.

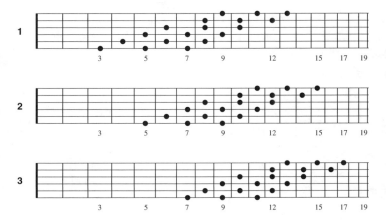

Diminished

The diminished scale comes in two varieties: the whole-half and half-whole. Both are atonal, with every second note spelling out a diminished 7th arpeggio.

Whole-half

The whole-half scale is a sequence of repeating whole and half steps. The notes, tones, and intervallic structure are shown below on E.

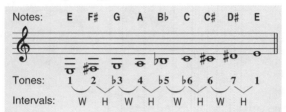

Below are positional and diagonal shapes for the G whole-half diminished scale. Similar to the idea in the whole tone scale, each can be shifted in increments of *three* frets without altering the pattern or tonality. Therefore, these effectively cover the entire neck.

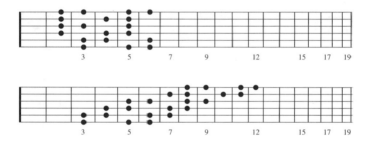

Half-whole

The half-whole scale simply reverses the pattern of half and whole steps. The notes, tones, and intervallic structure are shown below on E. (Every second note still spells the E diminished 7th arpeggio as above).

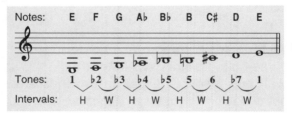

Below are positional and diagonal shapes for the G half-whole diminished scale. Again, each can be shifted in increments of *three frets* at a time without altering the pattern or tonality. Therefore, these effectively cover the entire neck.

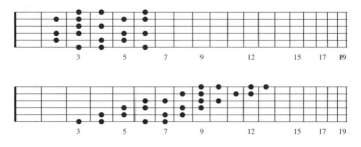

Other Exotic and Ethnic Scales

What would an ultimate scale book be without a bit of the unusual and bizarre? The adventurous guitarist may expand each of the following over the entire fretboard, as well as shift them into other tonalities.

Enigmatic

The structure of the enigmatic scale is shown below on C. It begins like Phrygian-dominant, borrows the middle portion of the whole-tone scale, and tops it off with half steps around the root.

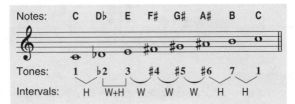

Below, the enigmatic scale's positional and diagonal patterns are based on A. Practice in other keys, too.

Double harmonic

The double harmonic scale features the bottom half of Phrygian-dominant and the top half of harmonic minor. Look in the structure for two W+H intervals flanked on either side by half steps. This structure is also known as the "gypsy" and "Byzantine" scale.

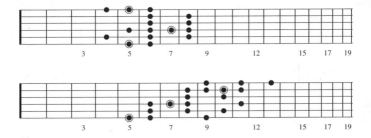

Below, the double harmonic scale is shown in positional and diagonal shapes based on A. Practice in other keys, too.

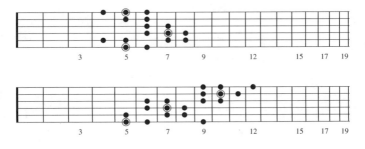

Hungarian minor

This is a harmonic minor with a raised 4th. Notice the W+H intervals flanked by half steps in two places.

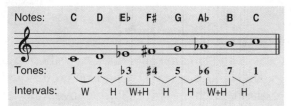

Below, the Hungarian minor scale is shown in positional and diagonal shapes based on A.

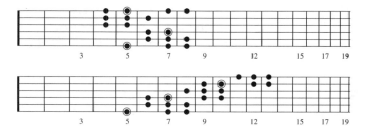

Persian

The Persian scale begins like Phrygian-dominant, then goes into a sort of "Locrian-harmonic minor."

Here is the Persian scale in positional and diagonal shapes based on A.

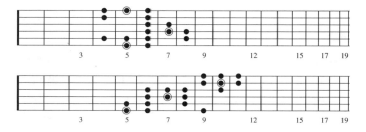

Arabian

The Arabian scale blends major on the lower half with Locrian on the upper half. (This structure may also be called the "major Locrian scale.")

Below, the Arabian scale's positional and diagonal shapes are shown based on A.

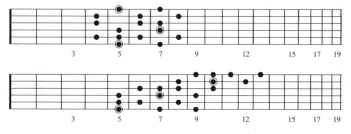

Japanese

This pentatonic scale has no 3rd, but a ♭6 and ♭2 give it an overall minor color.

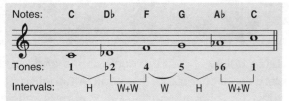

Below are positional and diagonal shapes for the A Japanese scale.

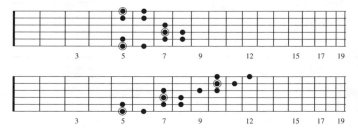

Egyptian

Here is another pentatonic scale with no third. It tends to lack resolution, and sounds odd as a key center. (It also happens to be the third mode of minor pentatonic.)

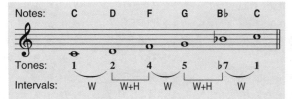

Below, the Egyptian scale is shown in positional and diagonal shapes based on A.

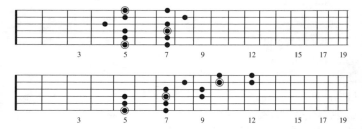

Hirajoshi

Another pentatonic scale, this one alters a major pentatonic structure with minor 3rd and minor 6th intervals.

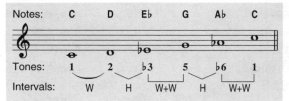

The Hirajoshi scale in A is shown below in its positional and diagonal shapes.

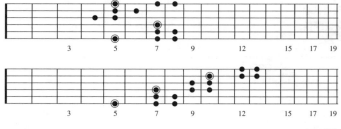

Appendix A
Scale Construction Table

The table below shows the scale tones and structure for every scale covered in this book. Alternative names are shown in parentheses. Tonal numbers reflect the note's position in relation to the tones of the major scale. The letter "w" stands for an interval of a "whole step" (two frets) and the letter "h" stands for an interval of a "half step" (one fret).

Scale name	Tones	Structure
major	1 2 3 4 5 6 7	w, w, h, w, w, w, h
natural minor	1 2 ♭3 4 5 ♭6 ♭7	w, h, w, w, h, w, w
major pentatonic	1 2 3 5 6	w, w, w+h, w, w+h
minor pentatonic	1 ♭3 4 5 ♭7	w+h, w, w, w+h, w
blues	1 ♭3 4 ♭5 5 ♭7	w+h, w, h, h, w+h, w
major blues	1 2 ♭3 3 4 ♭5 5 6 ♭7	w, h, h, h, h, h, w, h, w
minor blues	1 2 ♭3 4 ♭5 5 ♭6 ♭7	w, h, w, h, h, h, w, w
Ionian mode (major)	1 2 3 4 5 6 7	w, w, h, w, w, w, h
Dorian mode	1 2 ♭3 4 5 6 ♭7	w, h, w, w, w, h, w
Phrygian mode	1 ♭2 ♭3 4 5 ♭6 ♭7	h, w, w, w, h, w, w
Lydian mode	1 2 3 ♯4 5 6 7	w, w, w, h, w, w, h
Mixolydian mode	1 2 3 4 5 6 ♭7	w, w, h, w, w, h, w
Aeolian mode (nat. minor)	1 2 ♭3 4 5 ♭6 ♭7	w, h, w, w, h, w, w
Locrian mode	1 ♭2 ♭3 4 ♭5 ♭6 ♭7	h, w, w, h, w, w, w
harmonic minor (Mohammedan)	1 2 ♭3 4 5 ♭6 7	w, h, w, w, h, w+h, h
Phrygian-dominant (major Phrygian, Spanish-flamenco)	1 ♭2 3 4 5 ♭6 ♭7	h, w+h, h, w, h, w, w
Jazz melodic minor	1 2 ♭3 4 5 6 7	w, h, w, w, w, w, h
Dorian ♭2	1 ♭2 ♭3 4 5 6 ♭7	h, w, w, w, w, h, w
Lydian augmented	1 2 3 ♯4 ♯5 6 7	w, w, w, h, w, w, h
Lydian ♭7 (overtone)	1 2 3 ♯4 5 6 ♭7	w, w, w, h, w, h, w
Mixolydian ♭13 (Hindu)	1 2 3 4 5 ♭6 ♭7	w, w, h, w, h, w, w
Locrian ♯2	1 2 ♭3 4 ♭5 ♭6 ♭7	w, h, w, h, w, w, w
super Locrian (altered)	1 ♭2 ♭3 ♭4 ♭5 ♭6 ♭7	h, w, h, w, w, w, w
chromatic	1 ♭2 2 ♭3 3 4 ♭5 5 ♭6 6 ♭7 7	h ⋆ 12
whole tone	1 2 3 ♯4 ♯5 ♯6	w, w, w, w, w, w
whole half diminished	1 2 ♭3 4 ♭5 ♭6 6 7	w, h, w, h, w, h, w, h
half whole diminished	1 ♭2 ♭3 ♭4 ♭5 5 6 ♭7	h, w, h, w, h, w, h, w
enigmatic	1 ♭2 3 ♯4 ♯5 ♯6 7	h, w+h, w, w, w, h, h
double harmonic (gypsy, Byzantine)	1 ♭2 3 4 5 ♭6 7	h, w+h, h, w, h, w+h, h
Hungarian minor	1 2 ♭3 ♯4 5 ♭6 7	w, h, w+h, h, h, w+h, h
Persian	1 ♭2 3 4 ♭5 ♭6 7	h, w+h, h, h, w, w+h, h
Arabian (major Locrian)	1 2 3 4 ♭5 ♭6 ♭7	w, w, h, h, w, w, w
Japanese	1 ♭2 4 5 ♭6	h, w+w, w, h, w+w
Egyptian	1 2 4 5 ♭7	w, w+h, w, w+h, w
Hirajoshi	1 2 ♭3 5 ♭6	w, h, w+w, h, w+w

Appendix B
Note Names on the Neck

The vertical lines below represent the guitar strings, and the horizontal lines represent the frets. The low E string is on the left; the high E string on the right. The frets between the labeled notes are named with either a sharp of the note right below it (in terms of pitch), or a flat of the note right above it.

To play a particular scale in a different key than is shown in this book, simply find the appropriate root you wish to use on the diagram below. Then shift that scale's set of patterns up or down the neck placing the root symbol in the scale pattern on the new root note position. Play the same shape in the new position.

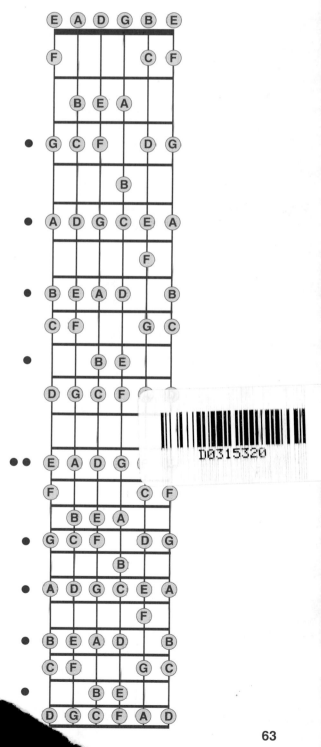